10-1432

$\mathcal{P}$resented to: _____

$\mathcal{F}$rom: _____

$\mathcal{D}$ate: _____

Cherished Thoughts on Friendship
Copyright 1998 by Zondervan Publishing House
ISBN 0-310-97744-4

Requests for information should be addressed to:

🏭 ZondervanPublishingHouse
Mail Drop B20
Grand Rapids, Michigan 49530
http://www.zondervan.com

Director of Gift Product: Gwen Ellis
Designer: Cris Gannon
Compiler: Judith Couchman

Judith Couchman is the owner of Judith & Company and works as an author, editor, and speaker. She is the author/compiler of twenty-six books and lives in Colorado.

99 00 01 02 /HK/ 5 4 3 2

Printed in China

Cherished Thoughts...

F·on riendship

Zondervan *Gifts*
We have a gift for inspiration™

$\mathcal{B}$e completely
humble and gentle;
be patient, bearing
with one another
in love.

—*EPHESIANS 4:2*

*F*ortify yourself with a flock of friends! You can select them at random, write to one, dine with one, visit one, or take your problems to one. There is always at least one who will understand, inspire, and give you the lift you need at you need at the time.

—GEORGE MATTHEW ADAMS

$\mathcal{M}$y intercessor is my friend as my eyes pour out tears to God.

—JOB 16:20

$\mathcal{F}$riendship improves happiness and abates misery by doubling our joy and dividing our grief.

—JOSEPH ADDISON

A doubtful friend is worse than a certain enemy. Let a man be one thing or the other, and we then know how to meet him.

—AESOP

I will say,
"Peace be
within you."

—PSALM 122:8

*M*y friend will tell me my faults in private.

—Anonymous

*W*ithout friends, no one would choose to live, though he had all other goods.

—Aristotle

How good and pleasant it is
when brothers live together
in unity!

—*Psalm 133:1*

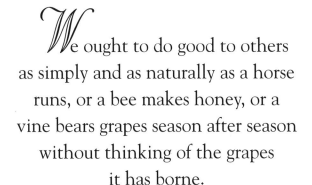

$\mathcal{W}$e ought to do good to others
as simply and as naturally as a horse
runs, or a bee makes honey, or a
vine bears grapes season after season
without thinking of the grapes
it has borne.

—MARCUS AURELIUS

$\mathcal{L}$et love and
faithfulness never
leave you.

—PROVERBS 3:3

$\mathcal{A}$ true friend will not always agree with you, but will be true to your best interests.

—NICOLE BEALE

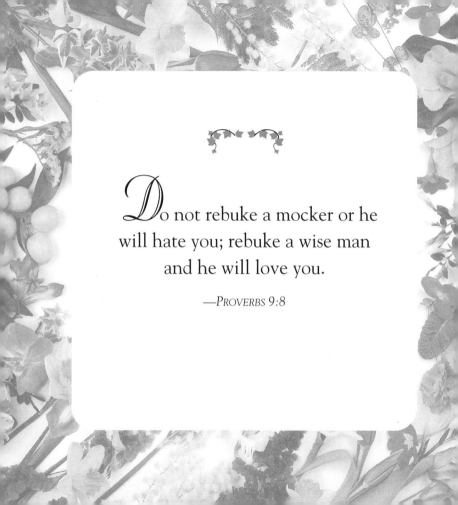

Do not rebuke a mocker or he
will hate you; rebuke a wise man
and he will love you.

—PROVERBS 9:8

From quiet homes and first
beginning,
Out to the undiscovered ends,
There's nothing worth the wear of
winning,
But laughter and the love of friends.

—HILAIRE BELLOC

$\mathcal{L}$ove covers
over all wrongs.

—PROVERBS 10:12

$\mathcal{W}$e cannot tell the precise moment when friendship is formed. As in filling a vessel drop by drop there is at last a drop which makes it run over, so in a series of kindnesses there is at last one which makes the heart run over.

—JAMES BOSWELL

*B*etter a meal of vegetables
where there is love than a fattened
calf with hatred.

—PROVERBS 15:17

A friendship can weather most things and thrive in thin soil—but it needs a little mulch of letters and phone calls and small silly presents every so often—just to save it from drying out completely.

—PAM BROWN

*M*ay the LORD's
unfailing love be
my comfort.

—PSALM 119:76

*Y*ou're my friend—
What a thing friendship is,
   world without end!
How it gives the heart and soul
   a stir-up!

—ROBERT BROWNING

He who covers over an offense
promotes love, but whoever repeats
the matter separates close friends.

—PROVERBS 17:9

$\mathcal{N}$o life is so strong and
complete,
But it yearns for a friend.

—WALLACE BRUCE

$\mathcal{T}$here is nothing final
between friends.

—WILLIAM JENNINGS BRYAN

$\mathcal{T}$here is a
friend who sticks
closer than a
brother.

—PROVERBS 18:24

$\mathcal{F}$riendship is a strong and habitual inclination in two persons to promote the good and happiness of one another.

—EUSTACE BUDGELL

$\mathcal{H}$e who loves a pure heart and whose speech is gracious will have the king for his friend.

—Proverbs 22:11

Don't walk in front of me,
  I may not follow.
Don't walk behind me,
  I may not lead.
Walk beside me
  And just be my friend.

—ALBERT CAMUS

*W*ounds from
a friend can be
trusted.

—PROVERBS 27:6

$\mathcal{Y}$ou can make more friends in two months by becoming more interested in other people than you can in two years by trying to get people interested in you.

—DALE CARNEGIE

$\mathcal{W}$e are so very rich if we know
just a few people in a way in which
we know no others.

—CATHERINE BRAMWELL-BOOTH

$\mathcal{T}$rue friendship is Love
without its wings!

—LORD BYRON

$\mathcal{T}$reat your friends as you do your
pictures, and place them in
their best light.

—JENNIE JEROME CHURCHILL

Do not forsake
your friend and
the friend of
your father.

—PROVERBS 27:10

*F*riendship makes prosperity more brilliant, and lightens adversity by dividing and sharing it.

—CICERO

*F*riendships are
the ship the Lord
often launches to
keep my boat afloat.

—PATSY CLAIRMONT

*I*f one falls down, his friend can help him up. But pity the man who falls and has no one to help him up!

—*Ecclesiastes 4:10*

*F*riendship is a sheltering tree.

—*Samuel Taylor Coleridge*

*F*riendship that flows from the heart cannot be frozen by adversity, as the water that flows from the spring cannot congeal in winter.

—JAMES FENIMORE COOPER

$\mathcal{A}$s iron sharpens iron, so one man sharpens another.

—Proverbs 27:17

Do not save your loving speeches
for your friends till they are dead;
Do not write them on their tombstones,
Speak them rather now instead.

—Anna Cummins

*W*hen Jesus saw their faith, he said, "Friend, your sins are forgiven."

—*LUKE 5:20*

*F*riends are those rare people who ask how we are and then wait to hear the answer.

—*ED CUNNINGHAM*

*D*o not protect yourself by a
fence, but rather by your friends.

—CZECH PROVERB

$\mathscr{A}$ new command I give you: Love one another.

—JOHN 13:34

Friendship is a spiritual thing. It is independent of matter or space or time. That which I love in my friend is not that which I see. What influences me in my friend is not his body, but his spirit.

—JOHN DRUMMOND

$\mathcal{B}$y this all men will know that
you are my disciples, if you love
one another.

—JOHN 13:35

$\mathcal{F}$riendship, of itself a holy tie,
Is made more sacred by adversity.

—JOHN DRYDEN

The greatest gift we can give one another is rapt attention to one another's existence.

—SUE ATCHLEY EBAUGH

*L*ove each other as I have loved you.

—JOHN 15:12

*I*t is a good thing to be rich, and a good thing to be strong, but it is a better thing to be beloved of many friends.

—*EURIPIDES*

*G*reater love has no one than this,
that he lay down his life for
his friends."

—JOHN 15:13

To act the part of a true friend requires more conscientious feeling than to fill with credit and complacency any other station or capacity in social life.

—SARAH ELLIS

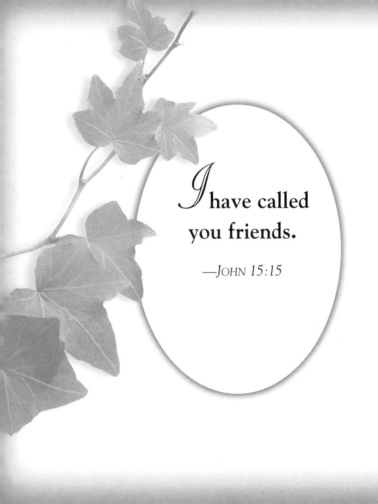

$\mathcal{I}$ have called
you friends.

—John 15:15

$\mathcal{A}$ friend is someone who can see through you and still enjoys the show.

—FARMERS ALMANAC

$\mathcal{B}$e devoted to one another in brotherly love. Honor one another above yourselves.

—ROMANS 12:10

$\mathcal{M}$y best friend is the one who brings out the best in me.

—HENRY FORD

*A*n enemy who tells the truth
contributes infinitely more to our
improvement than a friend
who deludes us.

—LOUIS N. FORTIN

$\mathcal{R}$ejoice with
those who rejoice;
mourn with those
who mourn.

—ROMANS 12:15

*N*o man is the whole of himself;
his friends are the rest of him.

—HARRY EMERSON FOSDICK

*B*e slow in choosing a friend, slower
in changing.

—BENJAMIN FRANKLIN

*L*ive in harmony with one
another. Do not be proud.

—ROMANS 12:16

*N*o man can be happy without a
friend, nor be sure of his friend 'til
he is unhappy.

—THOMAS FULLER

*T*rue friendship comes when
silence between two people is
comfortable.

—DAVE TYSON GENTRY

$\mathcal{B}$e careful to do
what is right in the
eyes of everybody.

—ROMANS 12:17

$\mathcal{F}$riendship is not a fruit for enjoyment only, but also an opportunity for service.

—GREEK PROVERB

$\mathcal{T}$he making of friends, who are real friends, is the best token we have of success in life.

—EDWARD EVERETT HALE

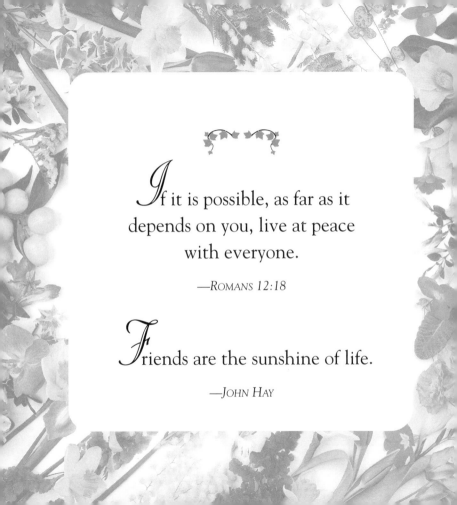

$\mathcal{I}$f it is possible, as far as it depends on you, live at peace with everyone.

—ROMANS 12:18

$\mathcal{F}$riends are the sunshine of life.

—JOHN HAY

*T*he best mirror is an old friend.

—GEORGE HERBERT

*F*riendship needs no words—it is
solitude delivered from the anguish
of loneliness.

—DAG HAMMARSKJÖLD

*L*ove . . . rejoices
with the truth.

—1 CORINTHIANS 13:6

The beauty of a friend is only a taste of what God is. It should be seen as an image of God, an enticement towards him. If the two spend their lives trying to look at each other only, they will never be open to the absolute fullness in God of which this friend is only a taste.

—PAUL HINNEBUSCH

$\mathcal{E}$verything we do, dear friends, is for your strengthening.

—2 CORINTHIANS 12:19

$\mathcal{W}$hy do people lament their follies for which their friends adore them?

—GERARD HOPKINS

A sympathetic friend can be quite as dear as a brother.

—HOMER

*N*ever while I keep my senses shall I compare anything to the delight of a friend.

—HORACE

Serve one another in love.

—GALATIANS 5:13

$\mathcal{A}$ friend knows how to allow for mere quantity in your talk, and only replies to the quality.

—WILLIAM DEAN HOWELLS

$\mathcal{B}$e completely humble and
gentle; be patient, bearing with
one another in love.

—*EPHESIANS 4:2*

*B*lessed are they who have the gift of making friends for it is one of God's best gifts. It involves many things, but above all the power of loving out of one's self and appreciating whatever is noble and loving in another.

—THOMAS HUGHES

$\mathcal{B}$e kind and
compassionate to one
another, forgiving
each other.

—EPHESIANS 4:32

*T*he friendship that can cease has never been real.

—*Saint Jerome*

*T*rue happiness consists not in the multitude of friends but in their worth and choice.

—*Ben Johnson*

*M*ake my joy complete by being
like-minded, having the same love,
being one in spirit and purpose.

—PHILIPPIANS 2:2

$\mathcal{L}$ife is a chronicle of friendship. Friends create the world anew each day. Without their loving care, courage would not suffice to keep hearts strong for life.

—HELEN KELLER

$\mathcal{Y}$ou should
stand firm in the
Lord, dear friends!

—PHILIPPIANS 4:1

$\mathcal{T}$rue friends don't spend time gazing
into each other's eyes. They may show
great tenderness toward each other, but
they face in the same direction—toward
common projects, interests, goals—
above all, toward a
common Lord.

—C. S. LEWIS

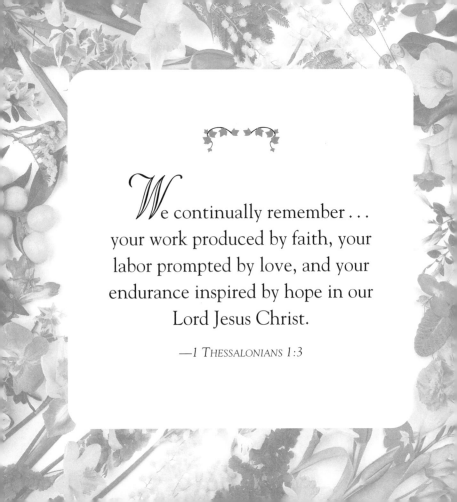

*W*e continually remember . . .
your work produced by faith, your
labor prompted by love, and your
endurance inspired by hope in our
Lord Jesus Christ.

—*1 Thessalonians 1:3*

The better part of one's life
consists of his friendships.

—ABRAHAM LINCOLN

*M*ay the
Lord make your
love increase
and overflow.

—*1 Thessalonians 3:12*

$\mathcal{I}$ always felt that great high privilege, relief, and comfort of friendship was that one had to explain nothing.

—KATHERINE MANSFIELD

*B*ecause the love every one of
you has for each other
is increasing.

—*2 Thessalonians 1:3*

*F*riendship is one mind
in two bodies.

—*Mencius*

The thread of our life would be dark, Heaven knows!
If it were not with friendship and love intertwin'd.

—THOMAS MOORE

$\mathcal{L}$ive in peace
with each other.

—1 THESSALONIANS 5:13

$\mathcal{M}$ay we not become so busy, harried, and overcommitted that we neglect the part of our soul that is fed and sustained by friendship.

—Marilyn Meberg

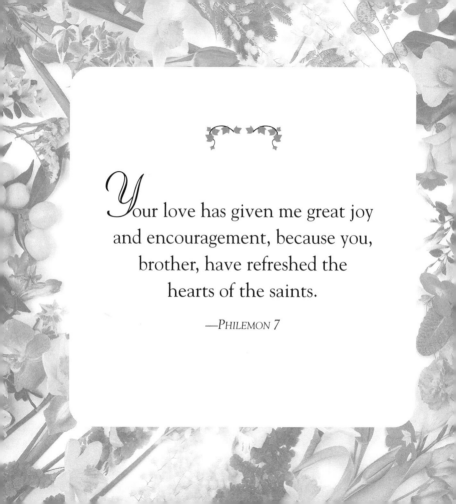

*Y*our love has given me great joy
and encouragement, because you,
brother, have refreshed the
hearts of the saints.

—*Philemon 7*

Whether you are blessed with soulmates . . . or with those who walk with you just a little while, not one of these [friends] crosses your path by chance. Each is a messenger, sent by God, to give you the wisdom, companionship, comfort, or challenge you need for a particular leg of your spiritual journey.

—TRACI MULLINS

Let
us consider
how we may spur
one another on
toward love and
good deeds.

—*Hebrews* 10:24

$\mathcal{T}$oo late we learn,
a man must hold his friend
Unjudged, accepted,
trusted to the end.

—JOHN BOYLE O'REILLY

*G*od will not forget your work and
the love you have shown him as you
have helped his people.

—*Hebrews 6:10*

*W*hen we express our gratitude
for others, important things happen
to them and us. We are renewed in
friendship and love. We are restored
emotionally and spiritually. And we
are inspired to learn how much we
really mean to each other.

—KAREN O'CONNOR

Let us encourage one another.

—HEBREWS 10:25

$\mathcal{Y}$ou can always tell a true friend: when you make a fool of yourself he doesn't think you've done a permanent job.

—LAWRENCE J. PETER

$\mathcal{L}$ove one another deeply, from
the heart.

—1 Peter 1:22

$\mathcal{F}$riends have all things
in common.

—Plato

*C*onvey thy love to thy friend as an arrow to the mark, to stick there, not as a ball against the wall, to rebound back to thee.

—FRANCIS QUARLES

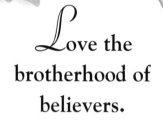

$\mathcal{L}$ove the
brotherhood of
believers.

—1 Peter 2:17

$\mathcal{F}$riendship with oneself is all-
important because without it one cannot
be friends with anyone else in the world.

—ELEANOR ROOSEVELT

$\mathcal{F}$inally, all of you, live in harmony with one another; be sympathetic, love as brothers, be compassionate and humble.

—*1 Peter 3:8*

*J*ust thinking about a friend makes you want to do a happy dance, because a friend is someone who loves you in spite of your faults.

—CHARLES M. SCHULZ

*L*ove covers
over a multitude
of sins.

—1 PETER 4:8

When true friends meet
in adverse hour;
'Tis like a sunbeam
through a shower.

—SIR WALTER SCOTT

*O*ffer hospitality to one another
without grumbling.

—1 PETER 4:9

*I*f I do vow a friendship,
I'll perform it
To the last article.

—WILLIAM SHAKESPEARE

*L*et us not love
with words . . . but
with actions and
in truth.

—1 John 3:18

$\mathcal{S}$o long as we are loved by others I should say that we are almost indispensable; and no man is useless while he has a friend.

—Robert Louis Stevenson

*E*ach one should use whatever
gift he has received to serve others,
faithfully administering God's grace
in its various forms.

—1 PETER 4:10

*T*o throw away
an honest friend is,
as it were, to throw your life away.

—SOPHOCLES

*E*veryone who
loves has been
born of God and
knows God.

—1 JOHN 4:7

Having friends around for a pleasant evening is one of life's most cherished joys as far as I am concerned. But when those with me are fellow believers how much greater that joy is, for we know that it will be rekindled, one day, in eternity.

—JAMES STEWART

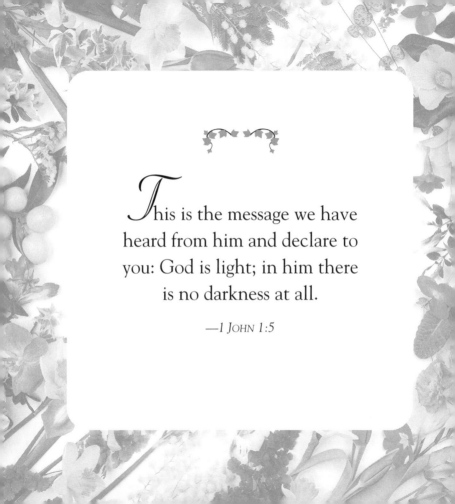

This is the message we have heard from him and declare to you: God is light; in him there is no darkness at all.

—1 JOHN 1:5

$\mathcal{D}$on't bypass the potential for meaningful friendships just because of differences. Explore them. Embrace them. Love them.

—*LUCI SWINDOLL*

I pray that you may enjoy good health and that all may go well with you.

—3 JOHN 2

$\mathcal{B}$y friendship you mean the greatest love, the greatest usefulness, the most noble sufferings, the severest truth, the heartiest counsel, and the greatest union of minds of which brave men and women are capable.

—JEREMY TAYLOR

$\mathscr{L}$ove comes from God.

—1 JOHN 4:7

If the first law of friendship is
that it has to be cultivated, the
second law is to be indulgent when
the first law has been neglected.

—VOLTAIRE

*Since God
so loved us, we
also ought to love
one another.*

—1 JOHN 4:11

One recipe for friendship is the right mixture of commonality and difference. You've got to have enough in common so that you understand each other and enough difference so that there is something to exchange.

—Robert Weiss

$\mathcal{D}$ear friend, you are faithful in
what you are doing for the
brothers, even though they
are strangers to you.

—3 JOHN 1–5

$\mathcal{T}$he only thing to do is to hug
one's friends tight and do one's jobs.

—EDITH WHARTON

Defining a friend is like trying
to define beauty: It's often in the
eye of the beholder.

—JERRY AND MARY WHITE

*M*ercy, peace
and love be yours
in abundance.

—JUDE 2

*A*nybody can sympathize with the suffering of a friend, but it requires a very fine nature to sympathize with a friend's success.

—OSCAR WILDE

But you, dear friends, build yourselves up in your most holy faith and pray in the Holy Spirit.

—JUDE 20

A friend is one who walks in when others walk out.

—WALTER WINCHELL

*T*hink where man's glory most
begins and ends
And say my glory was I had such
friends.

—WILLIAM BUTLER YEATS

$\mathscr{I}$am a friend to all who fear the LORD, to all who follow [his] precepts.

—PSALM 119:63

A true friend is the gift of God, and
he only who made hearts can unite them.

—ROBERT SOUTH

*T*he Christian should never complain
of his hard fortune
while he knows that
Christ is his friend.

—ANONYMOUS

When friends meet,
hearts warm.

—*Anonymous*

Inasmuch as anyone pushes you
nearer to God, he or she is
your friend.

—*Anonymous*

$\mathcal{F}$riendship is the garden
of God—what a delight to
tend his planting!

—INEZ BELL LEY

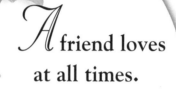

A friend loves
at all times.

—Proverbs 17:17

*M*ay the friends of our youth be the
companions of our old age.

—ANONYMOUS

*N*o good thing is pleasant to possess,
without friends to
share it.

—SENECA

$\mathcal{T}$rue friends weather the storm in
search of the rainbow.

—*EVELYN L. BEILENSON*

$\mathcal{T}$he wing of friendship never
moults a feather.

—*CHARLES DICKENS*

My friends are my estate.

—EMILY DICKINSON

Old friends are a comfort to the heart. Like a favorite robe and a familiar song, they wrap you in the warmth of their presence and you understand all the words.

—PAT MATUSZAK

I thank my God every time I remember you.

—PHILIPPIANS 3:1